True Bible Stories Vol. 1

BY MIIKO SHAFFIER
co-written by Chana Grosser

Illustrated by: Dmitry Gitelman (diemgi.com)
Layout & Design by: Ken Parker (visual-variables.com)

Published by:
Shefer Publishing
www.SheferPublishing.com

For permissions, comments and ordering information write:
Miiko@LearnHebrew.tv

ISBN 978-1-958999-11-0

TRUE BIBLE STORIES

VOLUME ONE

BY MIIKO SHAFFIER

SHEFER
PUBLISHING

Table of Contents

THE PROMISE OF THE RAINBOW

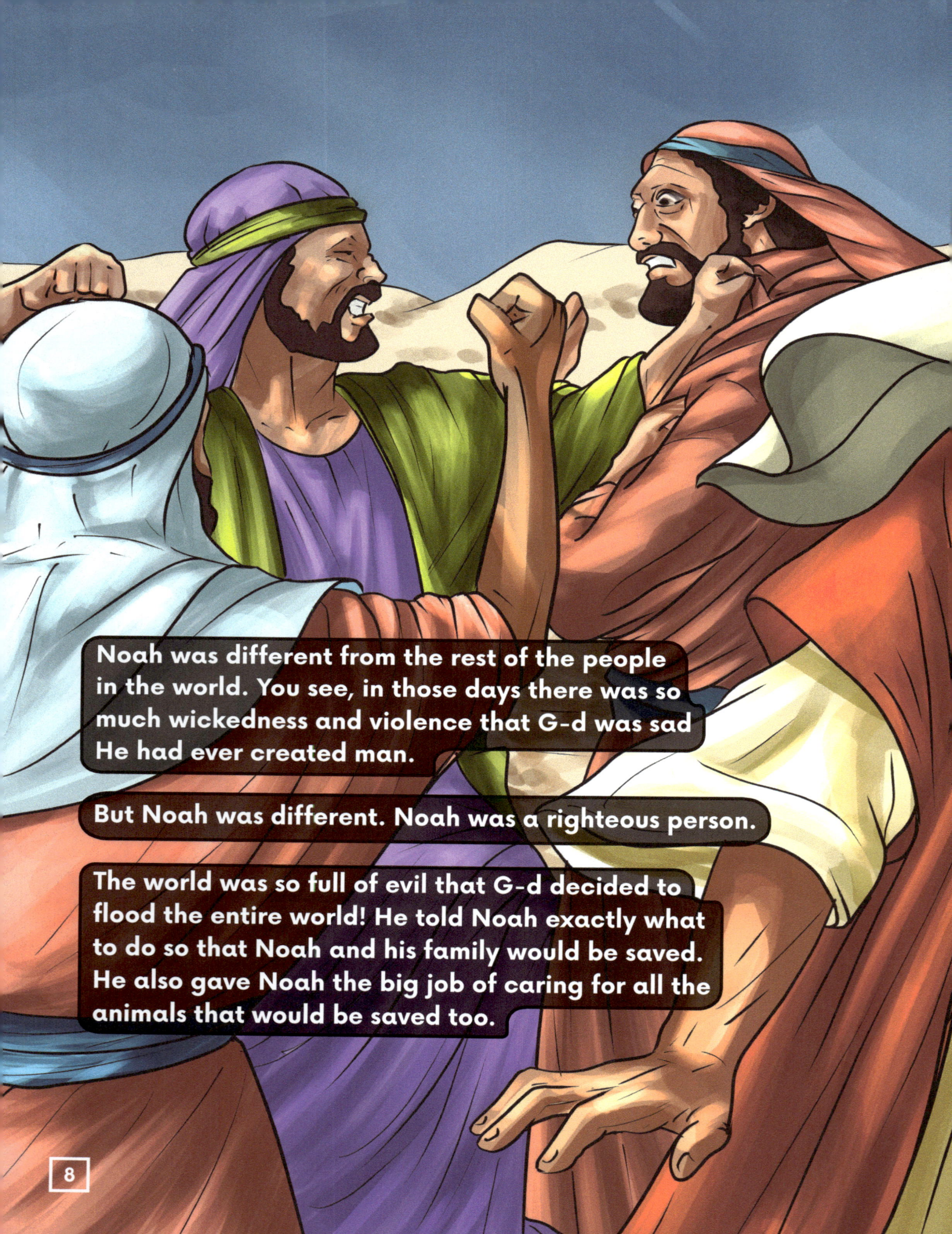

Noah was different from the rest of the people in the world. You see, in those days there was so much wickedness and violence that G-d was sad He had ever created man.

But Noah was different. Noah was a righteous person.

The world was so full of evil that G-d decided to flood the entire world! He told Noah exactly what to do so that Noah and his family would be saved. He also gave Noah the big job of caring for all the animals that would be saved too.

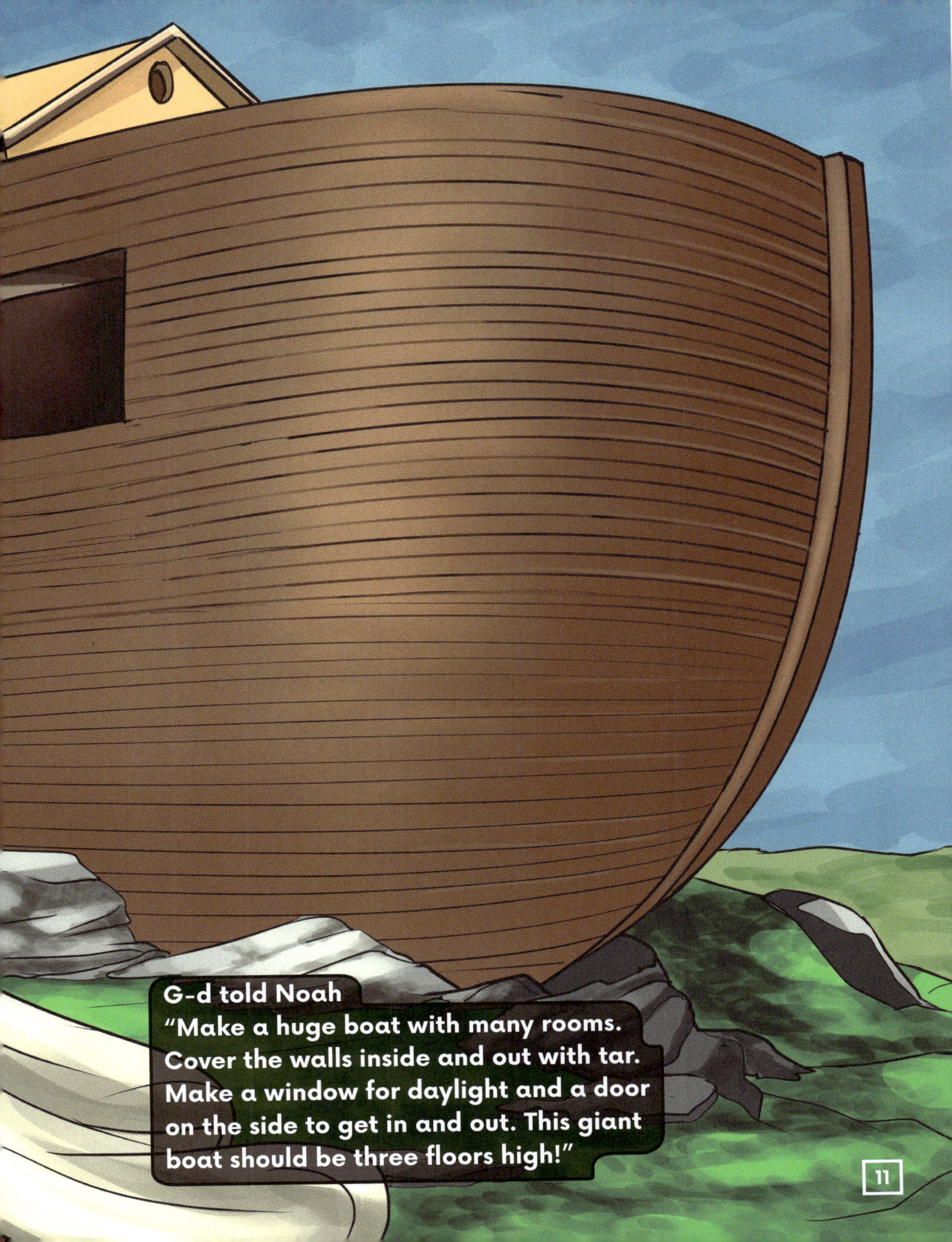

G-d told Noah
"Make a huge boat with many rooms. Cover the walls inside and out with tar. Make a window for daylight and a door on the side to get in and out. This giant boat should be three floors high!"

Noah worked on the boat for a long time. Part by part, stage after stage, Noah carefully worked.

Will the lion have enough to eat?
Would the birds forget how to fly?
Would all the noise and all the joys
Fit in this boat 3 levels high?

13

When the giant boat was ready G-d said to Noah: "I saw that you are righteous. Now you and your whole family need to go inside the boat you built. Bring the animals in too!"

"Bring the Kosher animals in groups of seven. Male and female. Non-Kosher animals in pairs. One male and one female. These are the only animals that will survive the great flood and they will be the beginning of the future."

This was a very big job and would take many days. G-d warned Noah:

"In seven days heavy rains will begin to fall. The rains will become heavier and heavier. And in forty days and forty nights the entire land will be underwater."

Only one week
Until the rains begin to fall
Only one more week
to check every corner and every wall
One last week
To call ALL the animals big and small.

Of course Noah came into the boat together with his wife. Noah's three sons Shem, Cham and Yafet came with their wives as well.
All these people came into the boat, and so many types of animals joined Noah and his family!

Giraffes and tigers, frogs and grasshoppers, pigeons and crows. They all went into the boat.

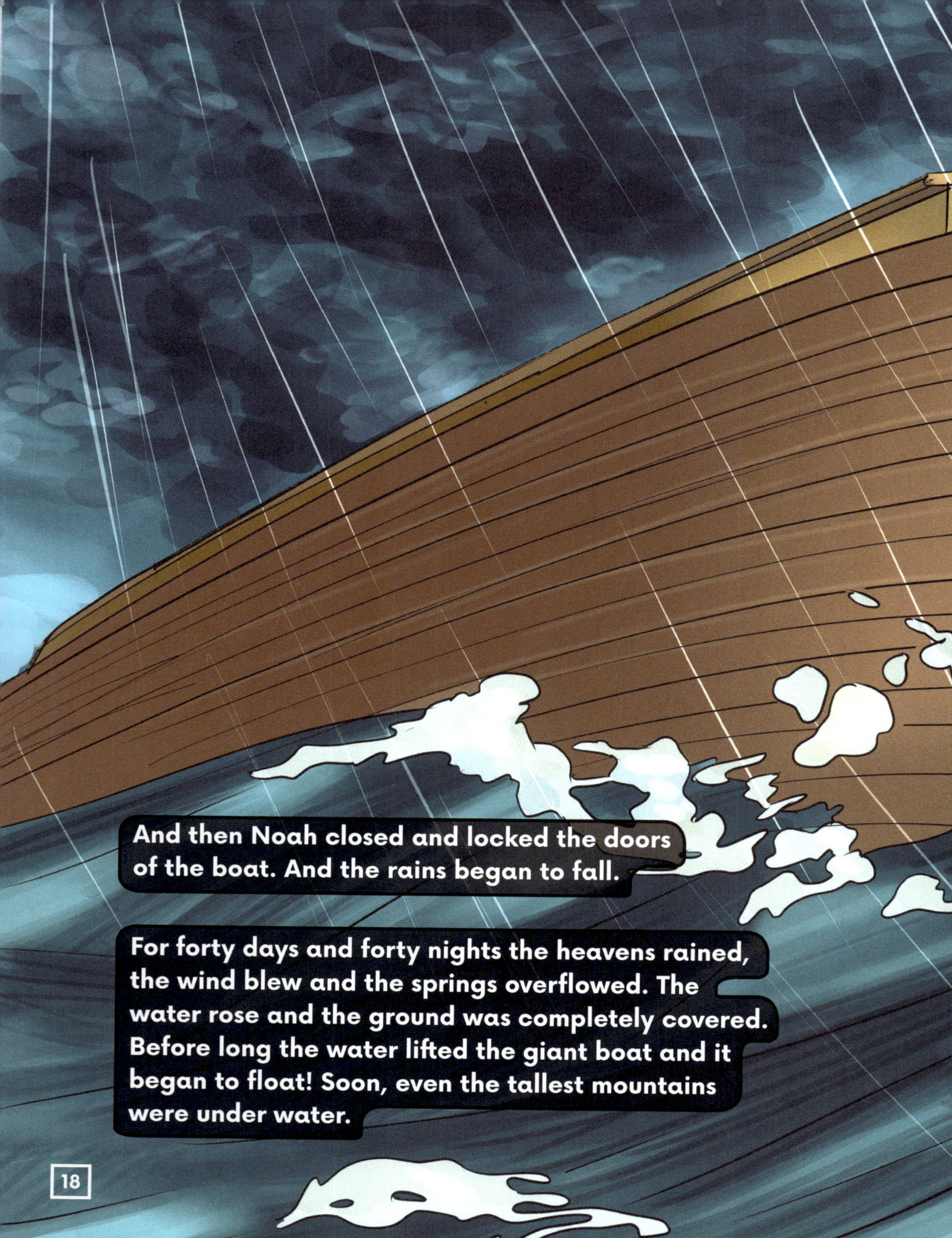

And then Noah closed and locked the doors of the boat. And the rains began to fall.

For forty days and forty nights the heavens rained, the wind blew and the springs overflowed. The water rose and the ground was completely covered. Before long the water lifted the giant boat and it began to float! Soon, even the tallest mountains were under water.

Then for 150 days the water swelled and rose higher and higher and higher still.

The only life in the whole world was afloat, in the great three story boat.
Noah and his family rushed around, taking care of all the animals who would have drowned.

And then something changed.

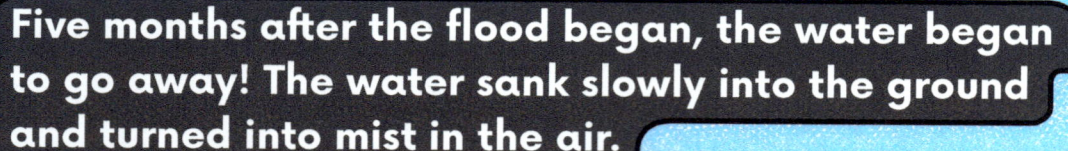

Five months after the flood began, the water began to go away! The water sank slowly into the ground and turned into mist in the air.

Thump! The bottom of the boat skidded and rested on the tippiest top of the tall Ararat Mountains!

After another three months, the shorter mountain tops were visible.

Noah threw open the boat window to look outside at the new world.

Then Noah gently brought the crow.
Little crow, little crow,
Tell us what you know.
Fly out through the window,
And see if something grows.
Noah wanted the crow to check if the
ground had dried enough for them to
leave the boat. The water had not yet
dried and the crow returned to
the boat to rest his tired wings.

Some time later Noah tried again.
Only this time he sent a dove.
Little dove, little dove,
tell us what you know.
Fly out through this window.
Has anything started to grow?
But the dove didn't even find a dry
place to rest, so she came back to
the boat.

Noah waited seven more days. He sent the dove out again. This time the dove returned to Noah with an olive leaf in her beak!

27

Noah waited seven MORE days. He sent the dove out again. Find a home! Fly away little dove! You will find Shalom! This time the dove flew out through the window and never returned. The water had dried!

One year and ten days after the great flood began Noah came out of the boat. His whole family came out of the boat. All the animals came out of the boat.

A colorful rainbow filled the sky. And so the world began anew. G-d promised there would never again be a great flood in the entire world and the beautiful rainbow is a sign of this promise.

THE
BRAVE JOURNEY
FROM SLAVERY TO FREEDOM

A new and powerful pharaoh stood looking over Egypt. As far as his eyes could see there were lush fields and sturdy homes. He could see the beautiful area where the Israelites lived, called Goshen, and he had a startling realization.

There are so many Israelites, he thought to himself. Before long they might be powerful enough to rebel against me! I need to use their numbers to Egypt's advantage.

"From now on," he commanded in a loud, harsh voice, "Israelites will work for the good of Egypt."

35

At first the Israelites were told to work in construction jobs and as farmers in the fields.

But despite their harsh life, the Israelites were blessed with many strong children. They became an even greater and stronger group in Egypt.

Pharaoh couldn't stop thinking about the Israelites! He couldn't stop thinking about how many they were and about how strong they were.

He looked at this people,
And knew what he desired.
"I'll pay them less to keep them poor...
I'll give them more work to keep them tired!"

The Israelites worked harder. Work that broke body and soul. Out of straw and mud they made bricks to build tremendous cities Pitom and Ramses.

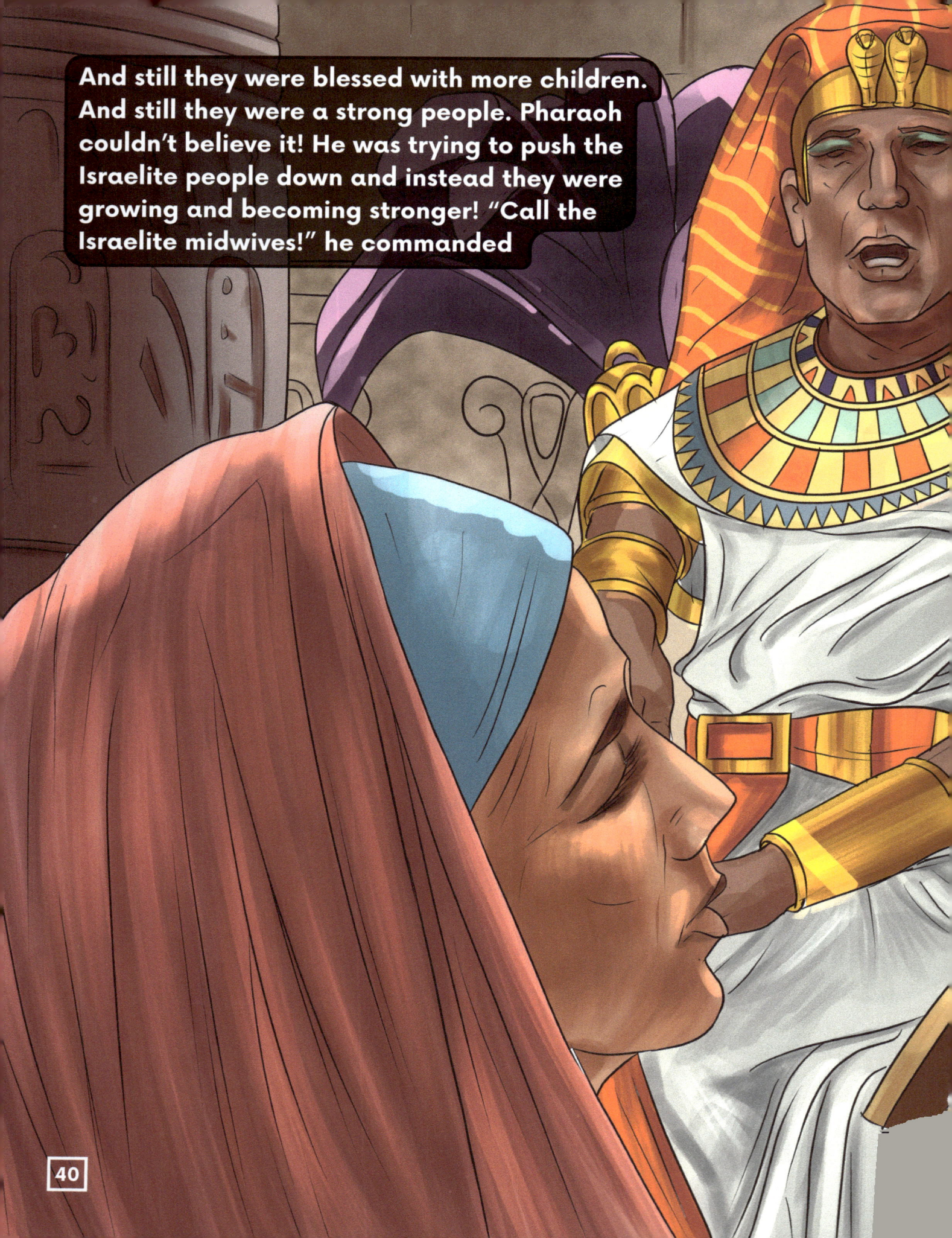

And still they were blessed with more children. And still they were a strong people. Pharaoh couldn't believe it! He was trying to push the Israelite people down and instead they were growing and becoming stronger! "Call the Israelite midwives!" he commanded

Shifra and Puah came right away. "When you attend the birth of an Israelite woman, pay attention," he said. "If the newborn is a boy, throw him in the Nile." "If a girl is born, you may keep her alive."

41

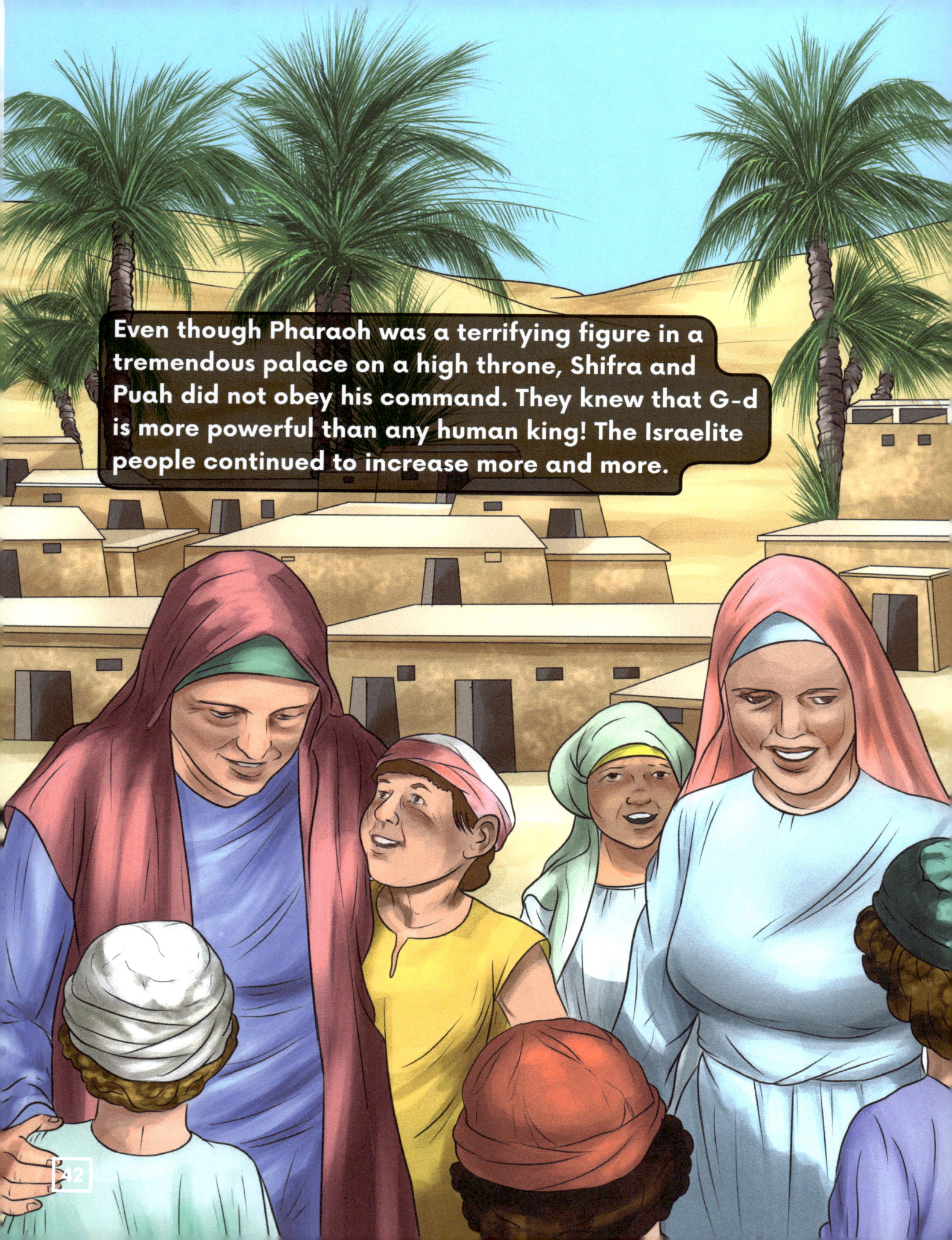

Even though Pharaoh was a terrifying figure in a tremendous palace on a high throne, Shifra and Puah did not obey his command. They knew that G-d is more powerful than any human king! The Israelite people continued to increase more and more.

Amram and Yocheved were a special couple from the tribe of Levi. They knew that Pharoah wanted all the baby boys to be thrown into the Nile . But just like Shifra and Puah, they knew that G-d is more powerful than any human king.

One exciting day, Amram and Yocheved had a new baby boy!
Their home was filled with light and joy.
For three long months Yocheved hid him well.
A family secret no one would tell.

But after three months the baby was too big to hide. How would Yocheved save her sweet baby boy? She thought of a plan and trusted G-d to help her.

Yocheved made a wicker basket. She lovingly coated it with clay on the inside so it would be smooth, and pitch on the outside so it would be waterproof. It was like a little boat. She called her daughter Miriam to help.

Yocheved put her precious son inside the basket and placed it among the reeds growing along the bank of the Nile River. She told Miriam "Watch over the basket with your brother. G-d will help!"

G-d makes the sun rise and the flowers grow.
He makes the birds sing and the Nile flow.
Surely He can save my beautiful brother, she thought.

Through the reeds, Miriam heard women's voices! Miriam's eyes grew larger as she saw Pharaoh's daughter Batya and her servants appear. They were coming down to the Nile to bathe. Would they be the ones to discover her helpless brother?

"What is that heartbreaking cry? Could it be a baby?! This must be an Israelite child!" said Pharaoh's daughter as she discovered the hidden baby.

Her compassion was greater than her father's order. She decided to save the boy in the basket and raise him in the palace as her own son. She named him "Moshe" which means pulled from the water. "Moshe" is Moses in English.

Miriam was still watching on the bank of the river. She knew this might be her only chance. With a confident voice she called out to the princess. "Would you like me to find a woman to nurse that child?"

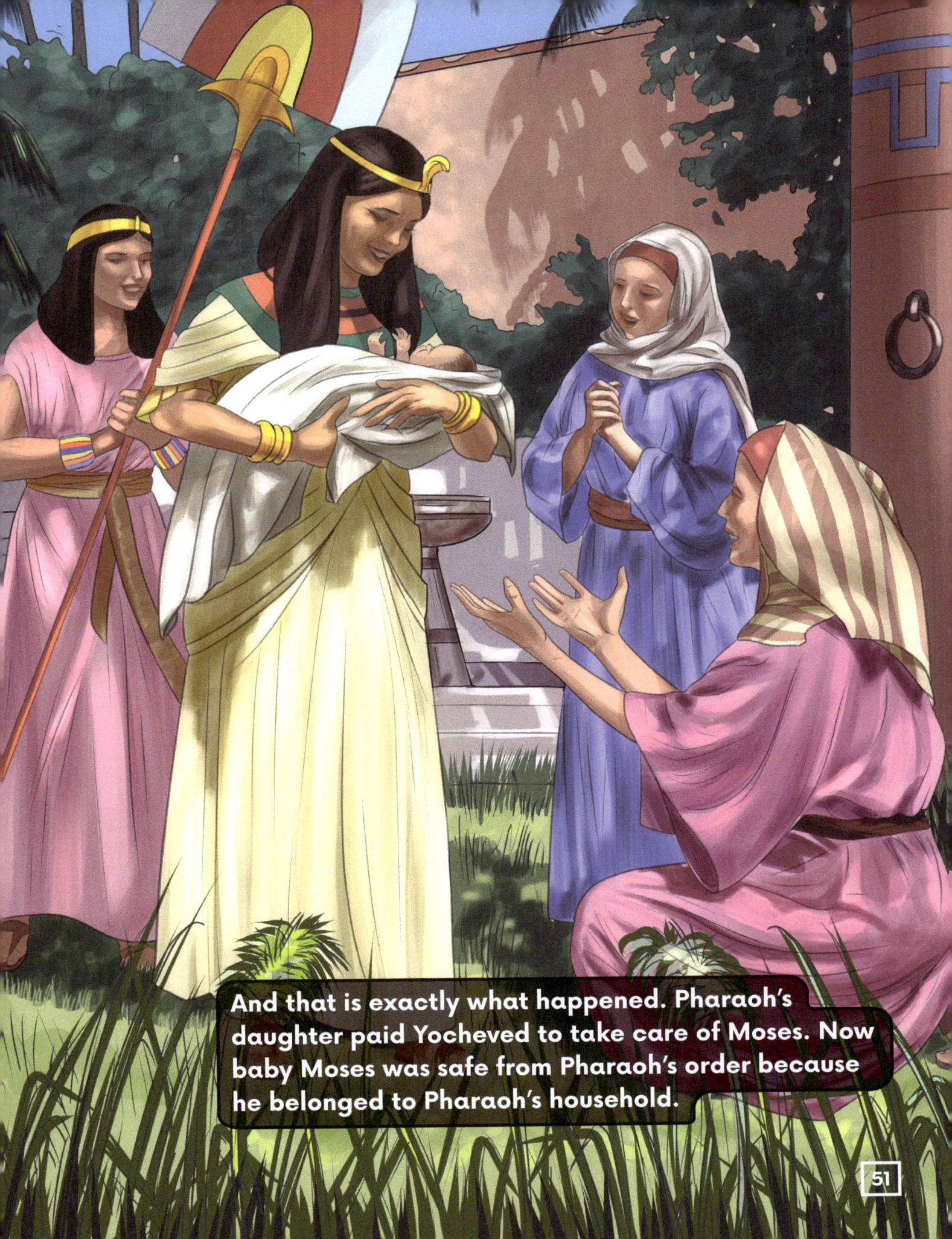

And that is exactly what happened. Pharaoh's daughter paid Yocheved to take care of Moses. Now baby Moses was safe from Pharaoh's order because he belonged to Pharaoh's household.

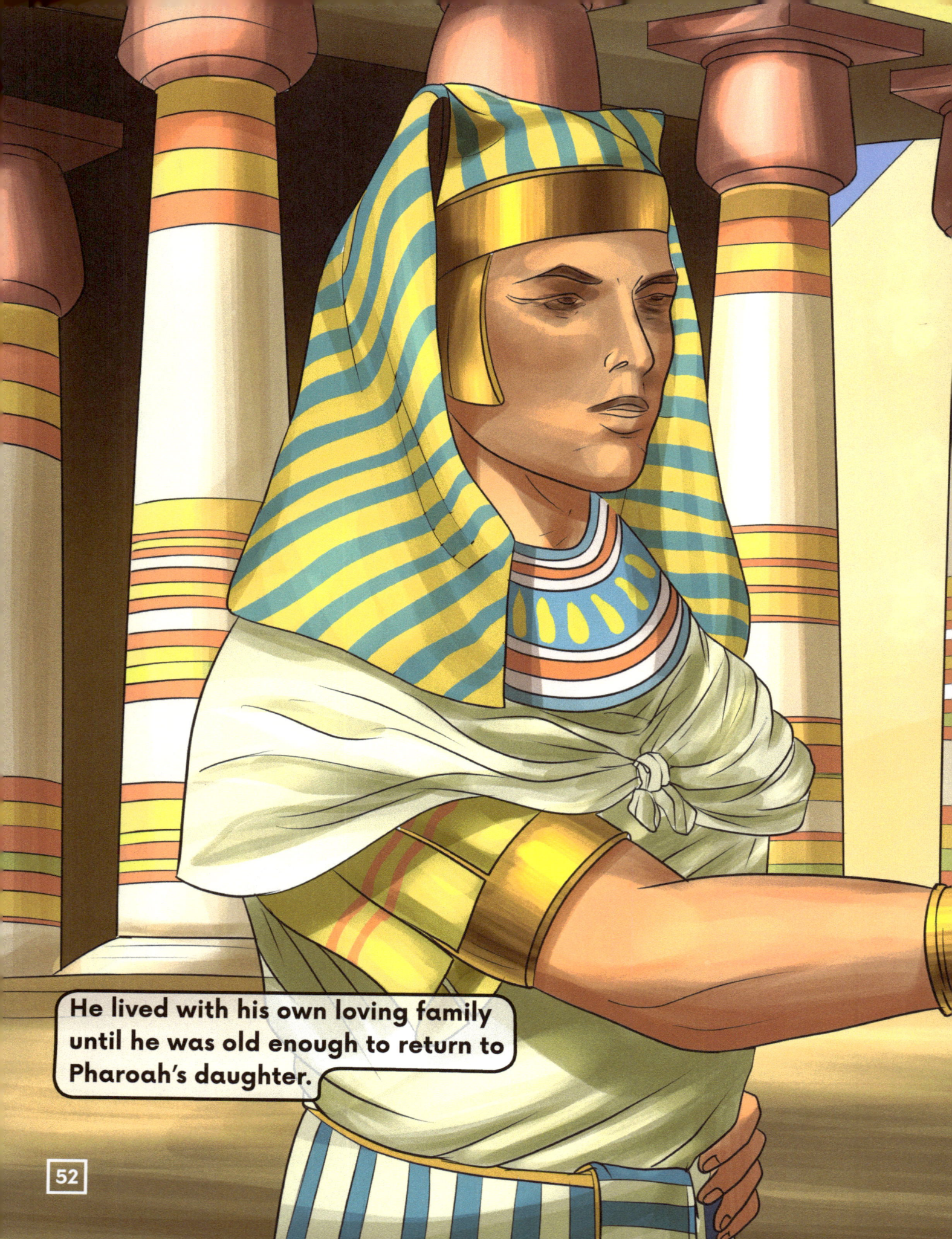

He lived with his own loving family until he was old enough to return to Pharoah's daughter.

He also knew that he was secretly an Israelite.

His people were outside, working harder and harder, for less and less pay. The Israelites had become slaves to the Egyptians and were whipped and beaten.

One day soon, with faith in the one true G-d, Moses would rejoin his people. His sister Miriam who watched over him as a baby in the Nile would be by his side. His brother Aaron would join him too. Together, with great miracles from G-d, they would confront the great pharoah and lead the Israelites away from the slavery of Egypt.

Where You GO I GO

A long time ago, in the land of Israel, in the city of Bethlehem, there lived an important man named Elimelech. Elimelech's wife was Naomi, and they had two sons.

Elimelech, like everyone else, suffered from hunger. Elimelech decided to leave Israel. He took his wife and sons and moved to the land of Moab.

It was not an easy step to leave, especially since he was a well-known and important person.

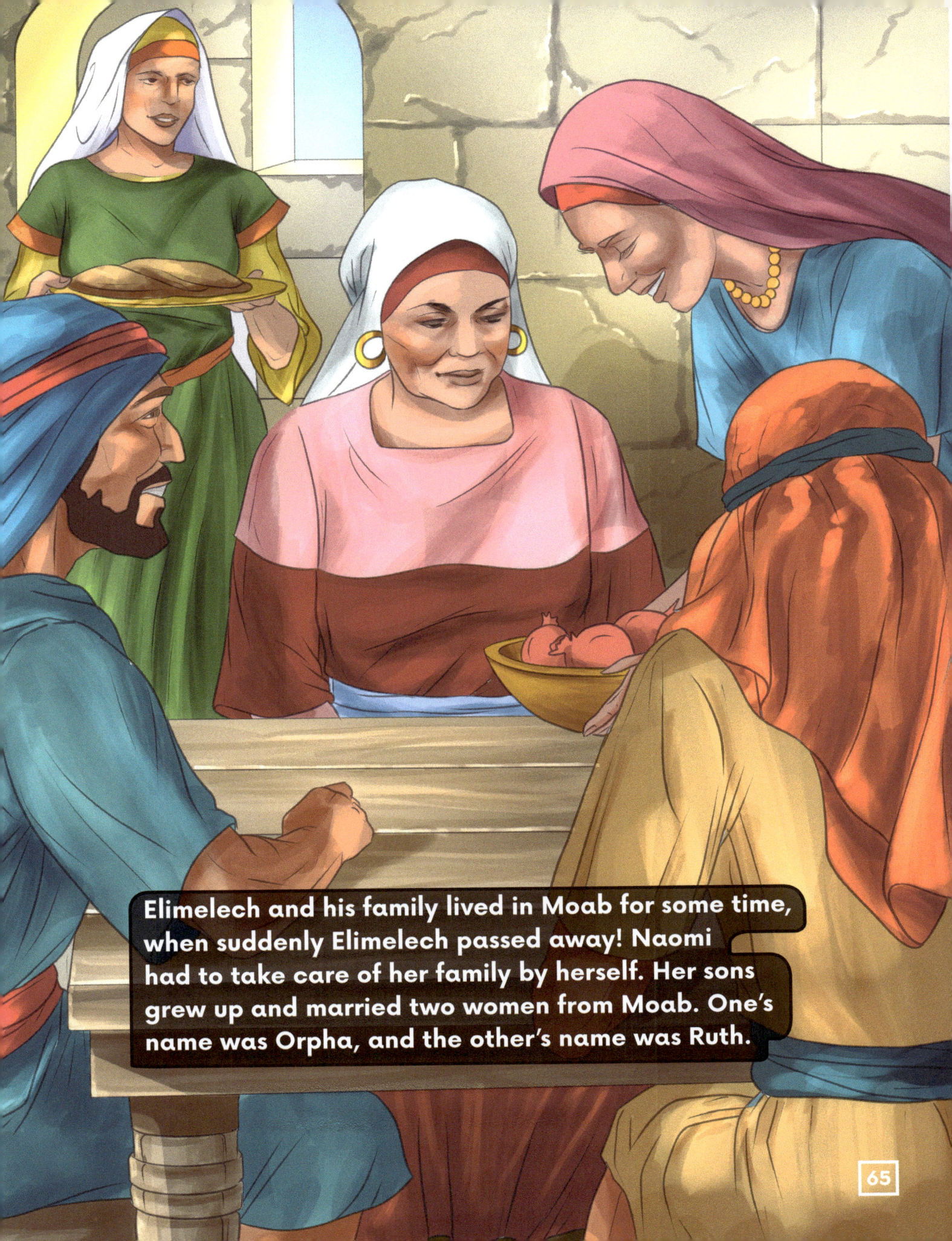

Elimelech and his family lived in Moab for some time, when suddenly Elimelech passed away! Naomi had to take care of her family by herself. Her sons grew up and married two women from Moab. One's name was Orpha, and the other's name was Ruth.

Naomi and her sons, along with their wives, lived in Moab for ten more years. But another disaster happened - her two sons both died as well!

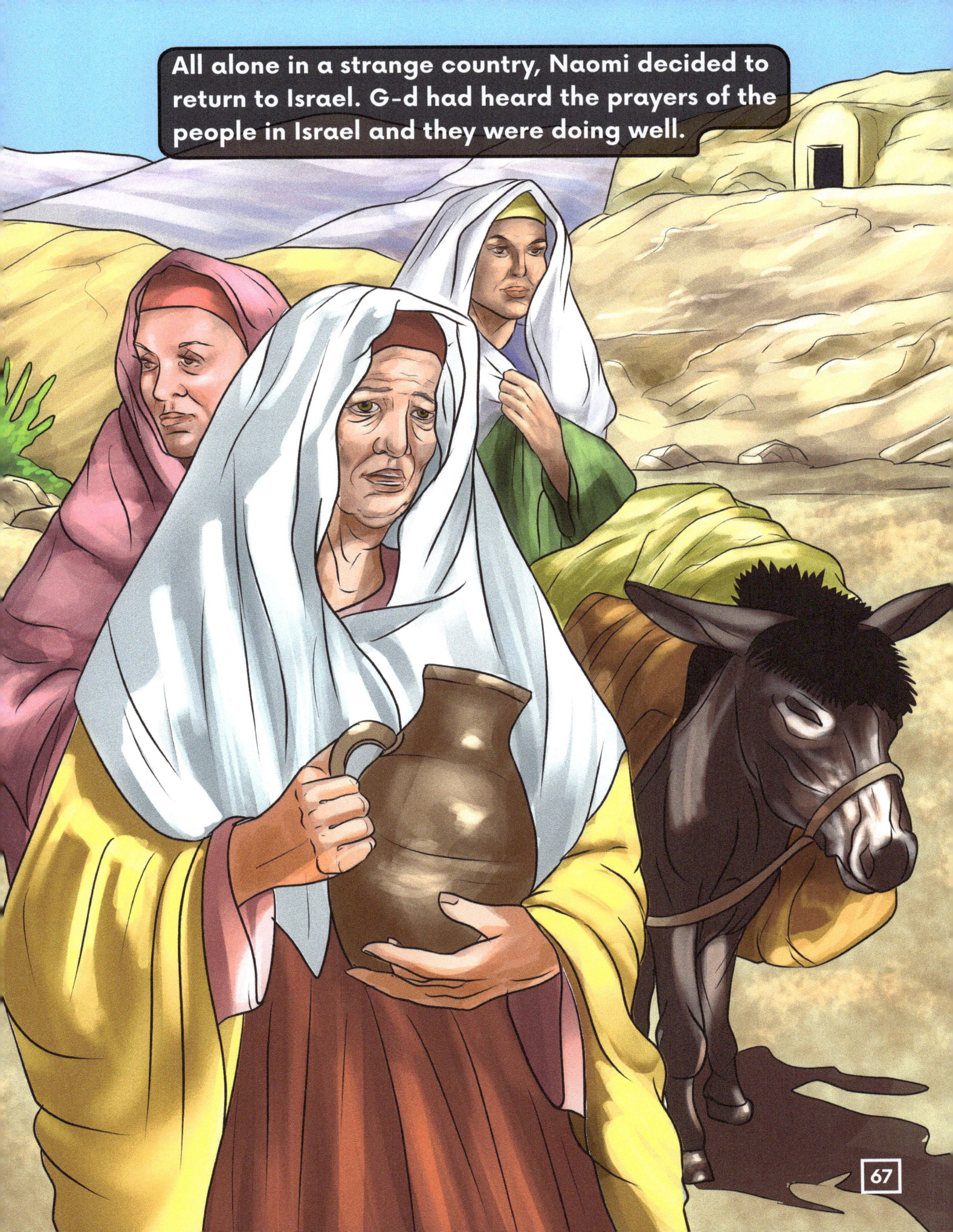

All alone in a strange country, Naomi decided to return to Israel. G-d had heard the prayers of the people in Israel and they were doing well.

Naomi found strength to continue because she knew that G-d sees the picture from above, And knows what's best for us with love, Though we may not comprehend, His plan is greater, from start to end.

Her daughters-in-law, Orpha and Ruth, began the trip to Israel with her. Naomi told Orpha and Ruth "Turn back. Go home to your mothers." But Orpha and Ruth refused to leave Naomi. Naomi told them again "Please, stay in Moab and find new husbands." Orpha turned back to stay in Moab.

But Ruth was a holy woman. She said
"Where you go, I will go.
Where you live, I will live.
Your people is my people,
Your G-d is my G-d.
Where you die, I will die.
I won't leave you."

70

Ruth knew that G-d sees the picture from above,
And knows what's best for us with love,
Though we may not comprehend,
His plan is greater, from start to end.

When Naomi and Ruth arrived in Israel, people were surprised to see Naomi and asked, "Is that really her?"

Naomi and Ruth were poor and cold,
They had no food, they had no gold,
But Ruth was brave, and strong and bold.

She went to a field with poor folk there,
To gather wheat with love and care,
And there she met a man so fair,
Boaz, the owner, kind and rare.

Boaz was especially kind to Ruth and even gave her more food than she needed.

Ruth told Naomi about what happened and Naomi was happy. Boaz was a relative of her late husband Elimelech. She told Ruth to continue collecting wheat in his field.

Naomi realized that since Boaz was a relative of Elimelech, and according to the rules of the Torah, Boaz could marry Ruth and buy Elimelech's land. Naomi encouraged Ruth to talk to Boaz.

Ruth went to see Boaz at night while he was sleeping near the fields. She asked Boaz to marry her, and he agreed. But first, he needed to check if there was someone else who had the right to buy Elimelech's land before him.

Boaz knew that G-d sees the picture from above,
And knows what's best for us with love,
Though we may not comprehend,
His plan is greater, from start to end.

Boaz did marry Ruth and bought Elimelech's land. Together they had a son named Oved, who would become the grandfather of King David. Naomi was full of joy and helped raise Oved as if he was her own son.

Naomi and Ruth raised the next generation of their family but also the future of the entire nation of Israel.

A VOICE IN THE NIGHT

In the hills of Ephraim lived a man named Elkana. A wonderful woman, Hanna, was his wife and he loved her very much.

To show Hanna how much he loved her, Elkana would bring Hanna lots of tasty food. But Hanna was sad. Too sad to eat the delicious food her husband brought her.

"Why do you cry?" Elkana asked his wife. "Why don't you eat?" "Why is your heart so broken?" Hanna was sad because she didn't have any children. No children to hold, no children to sing to, no children to make her heart happy.

She decided to ask G-d for a son. In her prayers she promised that this son would be a holy child, serving in the house of G-d.

G-d listened to her prayer and a beautiful son was born. His name was Samuel and he would be a holy boy.

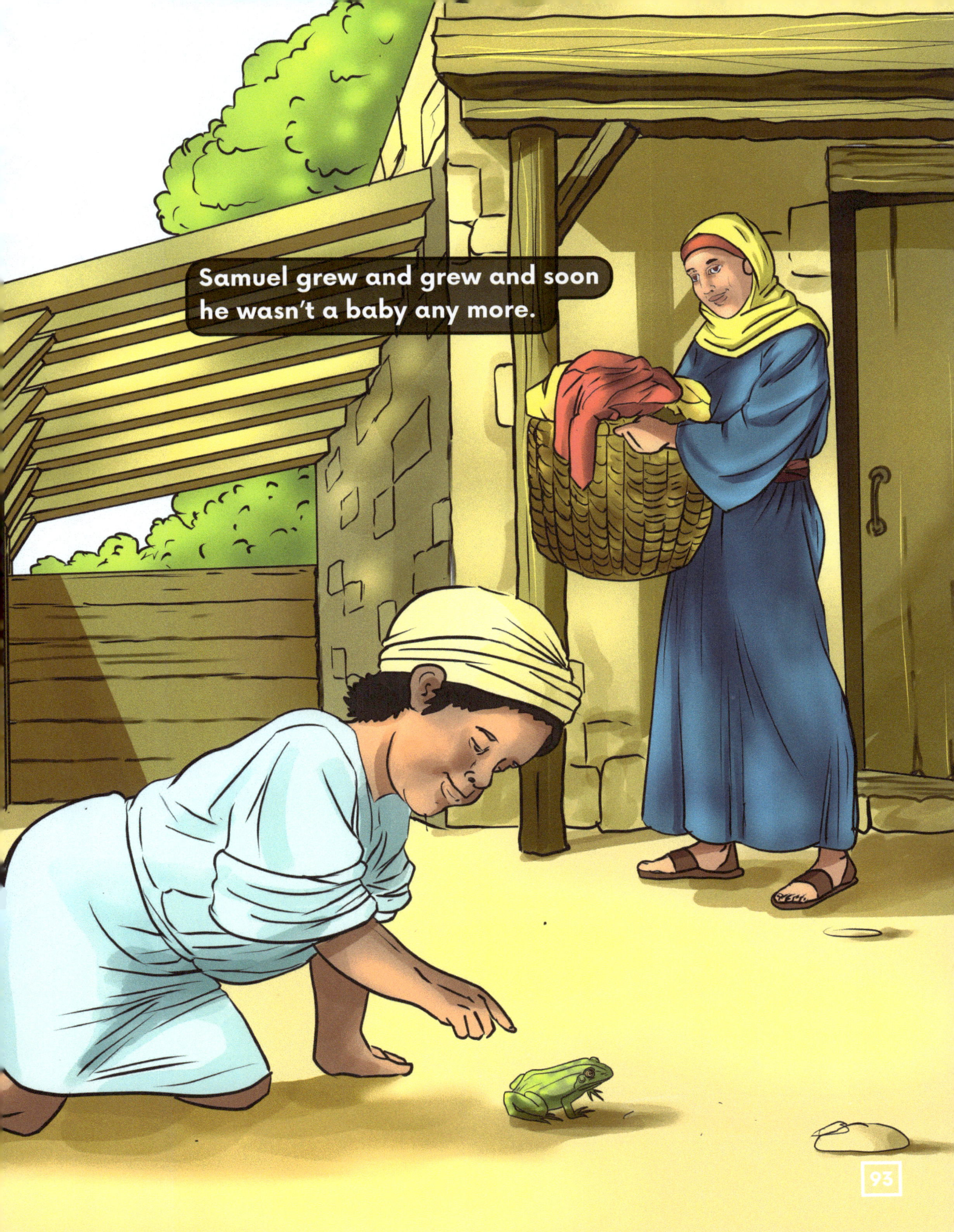

Samuel grew and grew and soon he wasn't a baby any more.

It was time for Samuel and his mother to go on a special journey. They packed flour and wine and took 3 bulls with them on their journey.

They traveled to Shiloh to The House of G-d. Samuel would stay in Shiloh. He would grow up with Eli the Great Cohen taking care of him in The House of G-d. One day Samuel would even hear the voice of G-d Himself!

Some visits brought a special surprise. On those visits a new baby brother or sister came to meet Samuel! Soon Samuel was blessed with three brothers and two sisters.

G-d heard all of Hanna's prayers. G-d saw all Hanna had done. He rewarded her with sons and daughters.

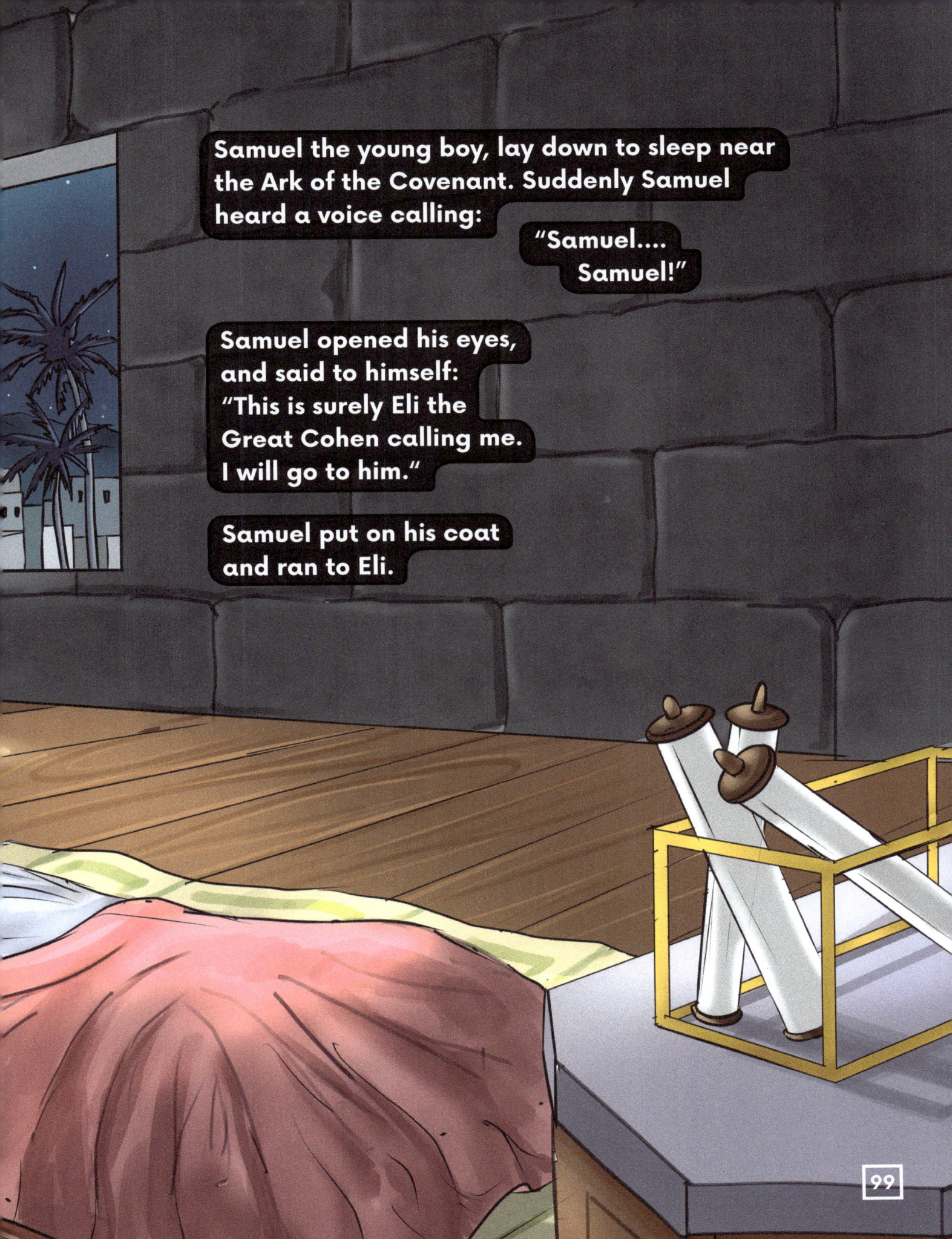

Samuel the young boy, lay down to sleep near the Ark of the Covenant. Suddenly Samuel heard a voice calling:

"Samuel....
Samuel!"

Samuel opened his eyes, and said to himself: "This is surely Eli the Great Cohen calling me. I will go to him."

Samuel put on his coat and ran to Eli.

So Samuel went back and took off his coat again. He lay down to sleep, again. The same thing happened a third time!

"Samuel.... Samuel.... Samuel!"

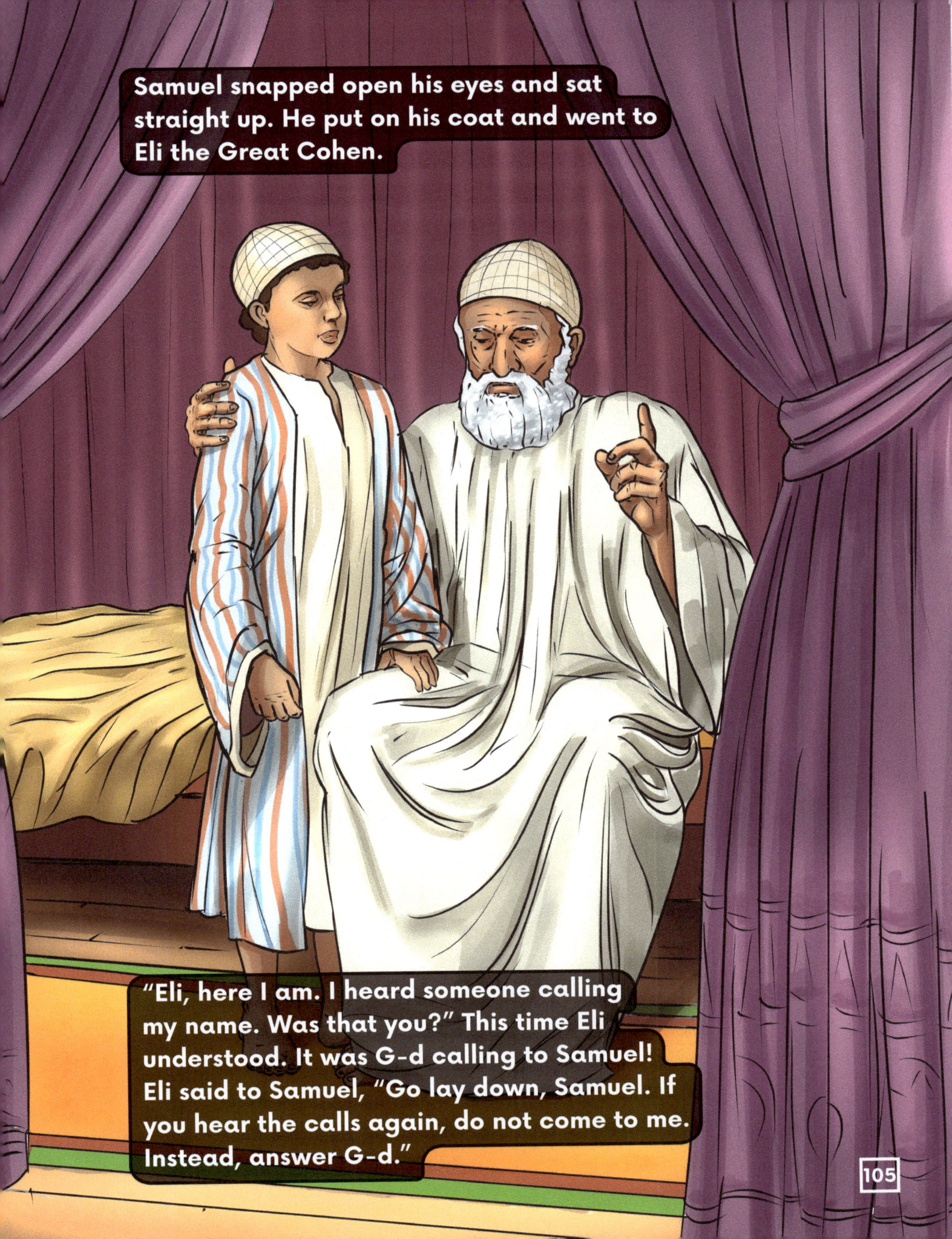

Samuel snapped open his eyes and sat straight up. He put on his coat and went to Eli the Great Cohen.

"Eli, here I am. I heard someone calling my name. Was that you?" This time Eli understood. It was G-d calling to Samuel! Eli said to Samuel, "Go lay down, Samuel. If you hear the calls again, do not come to me. Instead, answer G-d."

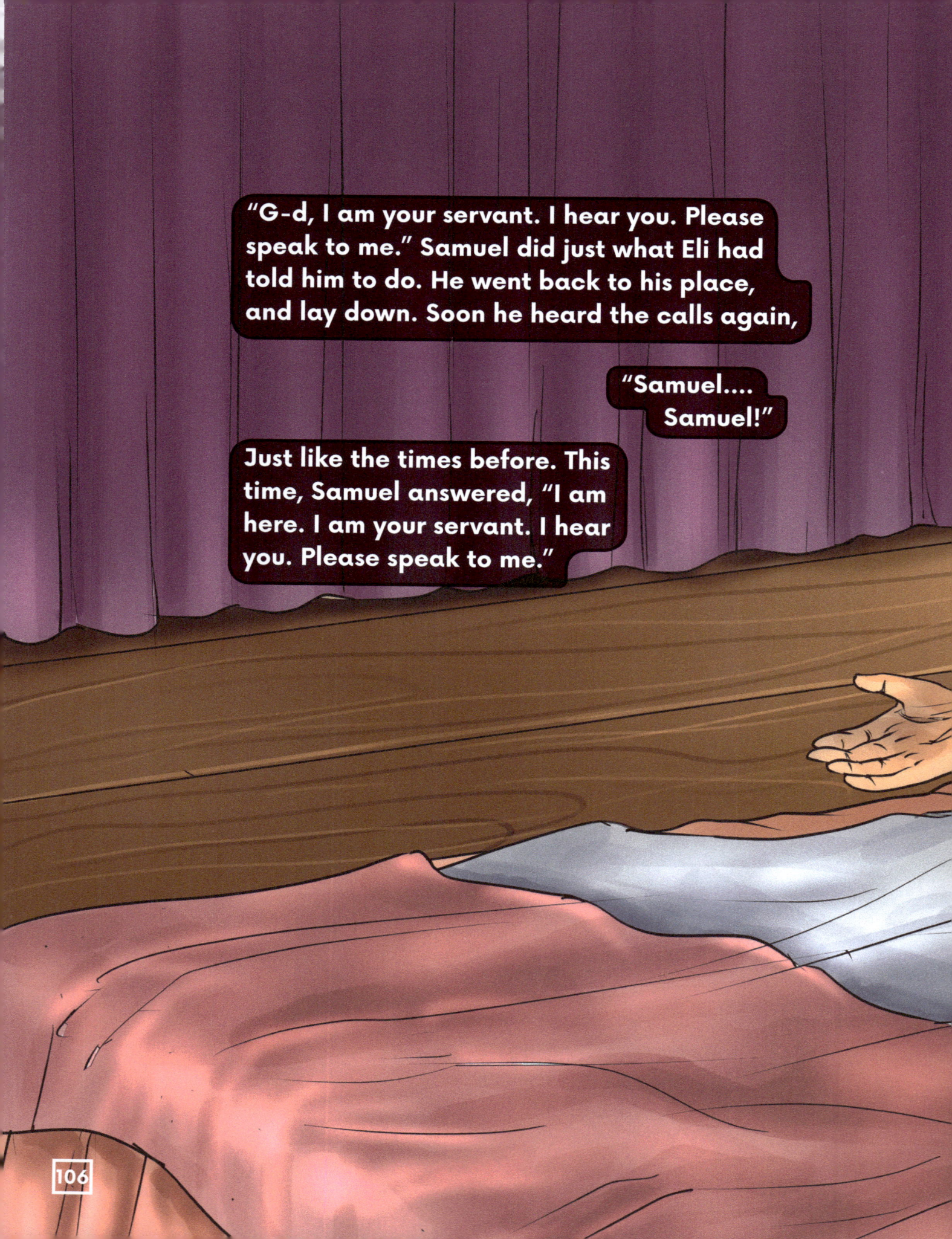

"G-d, I am your servant. I hear you. Please speak to me." Samuel did just what Eli had told him to do. He went back to his place, and lay down. Soon he heard the calls again,

"Samuel.... Samuel!"

Just like the times before. This time, Samuel answered, "I am here. I am your servant. I hear you. Please speak to me."

And G-d did speak to him! And that was how Samuel became Samuel The Prophet.

Samuel grew and grew and soon he wasn't a little boy any more. Everyone in all of Israel from Dan to Beersheba knew about Samuel. They knew that Samuel was a special and truthful prophet.

G-d would tell Samuel very important things. Then Samuel would tell the people in Israel all the important things G-d had told him.

One time G-d even told Samuel who to crown as King of Israel! Do you know who that king was? I'll give you a hint. He was very tall and handsome, had red hair and fought a giant gladiator named Goliath.

That's right! It was King David! King David and Samuel the Prophet went on many incredible adventures together!

THE
WIDOW
AND THE PROPHET

"Your husband has died, I know that! But he has left many debts. He owes me money! If you can't pay the debts, I want your two children. They will be my slaves. I will be back for either money or slaves."

117

The woman's husband was a G-d fearing prophet, and he had passed away not long before.

The woman knew he had left many debts. But what was she to do about her children?

This man wanted to take her two sons and make them his slaves!

The widow turned to Elisha, the great prophet of those days, for help.

Elisha told the woman, "Go to all your neighbors and borrow many empty dishes and vessels. Borrow as many as possible.

Then go home and shut the door. Pour oil from your jar into each vessel and set the full ones aside".

The woman did exactly what the prophet Elisha had told her. She went to her neighbors and borrowed many empty dishes and vessels.

Then the woman closed the door of her house. She started pouring oil into the vessels. The elder son handed his mother a large vessel made of clay.

The woman poured the oil and the oil dripped. The woman poured the oil, and the oil kept flowing!

It filled the vessel more and more until the vessel became completely full. The younger son took the small vessel and put it aside.

After filling vessels for a long time, the woman said to her son: "Give me another vessel."

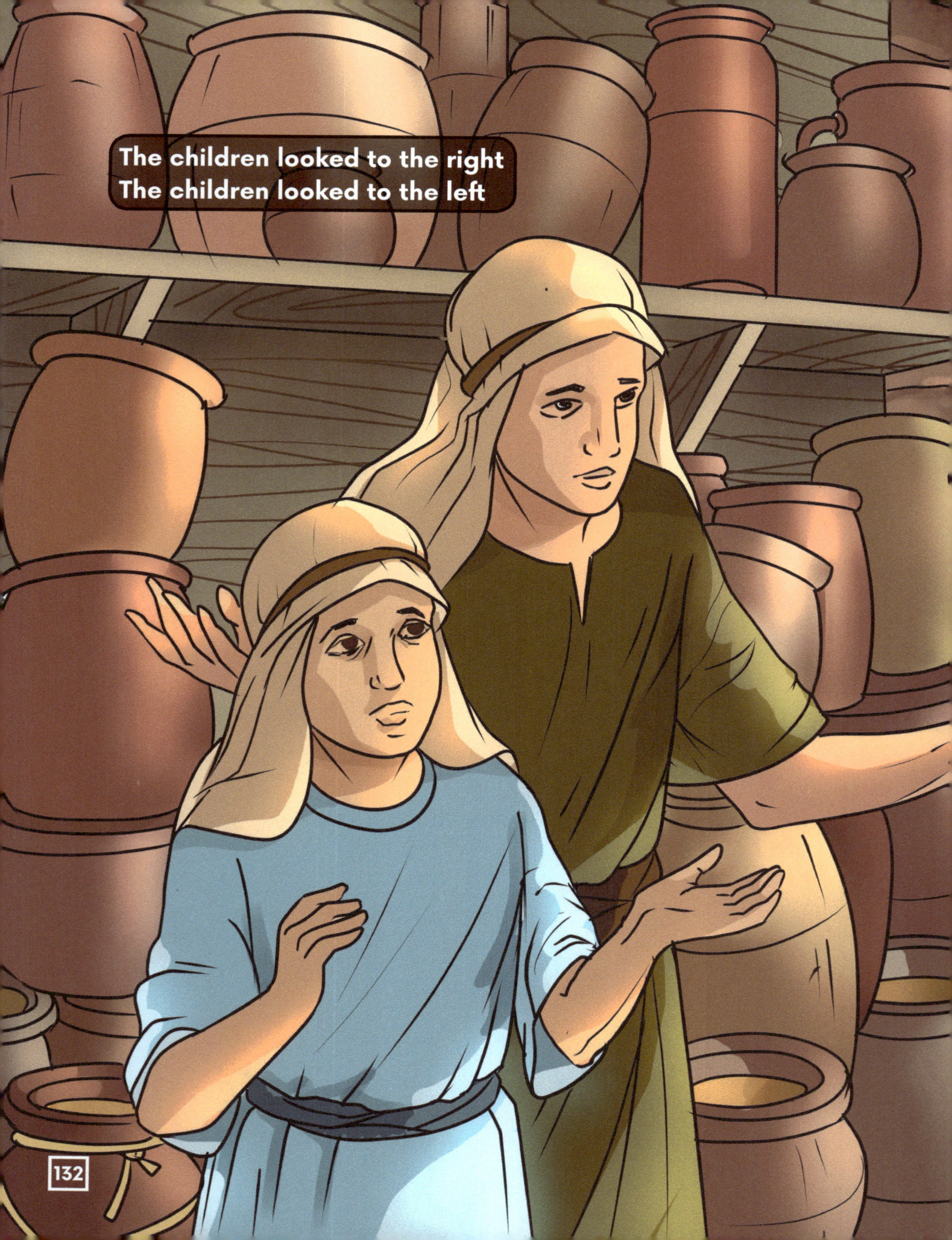

There were no empty vessels in the back.
There were no empty vessels in the front.
There were no empty vessels left at all.

So the son said to his mother: "There are no more empty vessels." And at that moment, the oil stopped flowing.

The woman went to Elisha and told him what happened, and Elisha told her: "Go sell the oil. The money will be much more than enough to pay the debts.

You and your sons will be able to live for the rest of your lives from the money that is left."

Hi!

I'm Miiko! I live in Beersheba, Israel, the city of Abraham. My husband Aaron and I are proud parents of nine awesome kids. I'm a Hebrew teacher for students of all ages, and Aaron is an Israel Tour Guide. We absolutely adore exploring Israel, soaking in the incredible places where the Bible stories happened.

FREE COLORING PAGES

SCAN CODE ABOVE

Because you bought my book, I want to gift you FREE printable coloring pages from True Bible Stories.

xo,

Miiko

www.ingramcontent.com/pod-product-compliance
Lightning Source LLC
Chambersburg PA
CBHW041513120626

46551CB00018B/2415